cooking the
NORWEGIAN way

Open-face sandwiches are a Scandinavian specialty that combines both familiar and unusual ingredients.

cooking the

NORWEGIAN way

SYLVIA MUNSEN

easy menu *ethnic* cookbooks

Lerner Publications Company ▪ Minneapolis

Series Editor: Patricia A. Grotts
Series Consultant: Ann L. Burckhardt

Drawings and Map by Jeanette Swofford

The page border for this book is based on a traditional *rosemaling* design called a *rosette band*. Another rosemaling design appears in the Norwegian fabric that is shown in some of the drawings. Rosemaling, or rose-painting, is a decorative folk art that was popular in Norway from the beginning of the 18th to the middle of the 19th century. Although it was done in many districts in southern and central Norway, the painters of Telemark and Hallingdal are the best known.

To my parents – the two best Norwegian cooks I know – with love and appreciation for sharing ideas and recipes

Library of Congress Cataloging in Publication Data

Munsen, Sylvia.
  Cooking the Norwegian way.

  (Easy menu ethnic cookbooks)
  Includes index.
  Summary: An introduction to the cooking of Norway, featuring traditional recipes such as fruit soup, Christmas bread, and rice pudding. Also includes a typical menu for breakfast, lunch, and dinner and several dishes from other Scandinavian countries.
  1. Cookery, Norwegian—Juvenile literature. 2. Norway—Juvenile literature. 3. Cookery, Scandinavian—Juvenile literature. 4. Scandinavia— Juvenile literature. [1. Cookery, Norwegian. 2. Cookery, Scandinavian] I. Title. II. Series.
  TX722.N6M86   641.59481   82-259
  ISBN 0-8225-0901-6   AACR2

Manufactured in the United States of America

3 4 5 6 7 8 9 10 91 90 89 88 87 86 85 84

CONTENTS

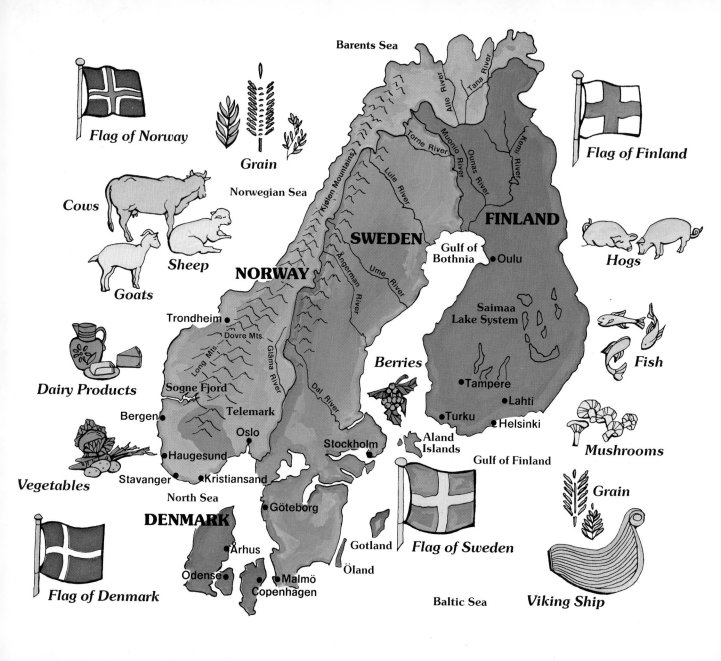

Flag of Norway

Grain

Flag of Finland

Cows

Sheep

Goats

Hogs

NORWAY

SWEDEN

FINLAND

Barents Sea

Alte River

Tana River

Torne River

Muonio River

Ounas River

Kemi River

Norwegian Sea

Kjølen Mountains

Lule River

Ångerman River

Ume River

Dairy Products

Fish

Trondheim

Dovre Mts.

Long Mts.

Glama River

Dal River

Sogne Fjord

Bergen

Telemark

Oslo

Berries

Gulf of Bothnia

Oulu

Saimaa Lake System

Tampere

Lahti

Turku

Helsinki

Mushrooms

Haugesund

Stavanger

Kristiansand

Vegetables

Stockholm

Åland Islands

Gulf of Finland

Grain

North Sea

DENMARK

Göteborg

Flag of Sweden

Gotland

Öland

Århus

Odense

Malmö

Copenhagen

Baltic Sea

Flag of Denmark

Viking Ship

INTRODUCTION

If you look at a map, you will see that Norway is shaped like a spoon. This is fitting because Norway is known for good food that is attractively prepared. In fact, many people lose no time in picking up their own spoons to enjoy it! Some Norwegian dishes, such as boiled potatoes and baked fish, are familiar to Americans. Other foods are new, but they are tasty to eat and easy to make.

The other Scandinavian countries of Sweden and Denmark, and the nearby country of Finland, are also known for their good food, so several recipes from these countries are included in this book. Although many of the same foods are eaten in these neighboring countries, it is interesting to see how their recipes differ. If you look at the three recipes for rice pudding, a familiar dish in each Scandinavian country, you'll see what I mean.

Because Sweden, Denmark, and Finland are each unique, a cookbook could be written for each of them. This book, however, is primarily devoted to the cooking I know best—the cooking of Norway. A quick look at Norway's land and dining customs will help you understand Norwegian cooking even more.

THE LAND

Water has always affected Norway's history and culture. This is because about two-thirds of Norway is surrounded by the sea, and it has hundreds of *fjords* (fee-YORDS) along its coast. A fjord is an arm of the sea that has carved its way inland through the mountains. Sometimes fjords are miles long. Since most of Norway is rocky and mountainous, the Norwegians have depended on the fjords and seas for both transportation and food.

Many Norwegians also depend on farming to earn their living, even though only about four percent of Norway's land can be used to grow crops. Family farms in Norway average only 10 acres, which is very small compared to American farms.

Norway has a very jagged and rocky coastline marked by long, narrow inlets of the sea called fjords. Pictured above is the beautiful *Sogne Fjord*, the longest in Norway. It stretches inland for more than 100 miles.

THE FOOD

Norwegian farmers grow rye, wheat, and barley on their small amount of available land. They also raise sheep, goats, pigs, and dairy cattle. Grain is used to make many kinds of bread, and livestock provides mutton, lamb, and pork, as well as the cheeses that Norwegians enjoy. A special Norwegian cheese is *gjetost* (YEA-tost), which is made from goat's milk.

Fruits and vegetables are other products grown by Norwegian farmers. This may seem odd since one-third of Norway lies above the Arctic Circle. But because of the warm Gulf Stream currents and mild southwesterly winds, Norway's average temperature is higher than that of other northern lands.

Norway is cool and damp during the growing season. Vegetables that grow well in that climate are potatoes, carrots, cauliflower, cabbage, peas, and rutabagas. Many kinds of berries thrive in Norway, too, including strawberries, blueberries, lingonberries (mountain cranberries), and cloudberries. *Cloudberries* are orange-yellow raspberries that grow in clusters. They are called cloudberries because they grow in the mountains in the south of Norway, "near the clouds."

Because they live so close to the sea, Norwegians eat a lot of fish. The waters surrounding Norway are rich with *torsk* (codfish), herring, and mackerel. And there are at least 150 salmon rivers along the coast.

In the summer, everyone in Norway can buy fresh fish daily at the outdoor fish markets. The most plentiful fish in the markets is *torsk,* which is practically the national fish of Norway. It is called "poor man's lobster."

Norwegians also preserve fish for winter. They salt and fry the *torsk,* or they dip it in lye. When it is soaked in lye, it is called *lutefisk* (LOO-tuh-fisk). Other kinds of fish are pickled, smoked, or frozen.

Although fish is certainly a major food in Norway, Norwegian cooking is known for its use of many different types of food. In fact, the Vikings (700 to 1000 A.D.), the early seagoing Norwegians, are said by some people to have started the *smørgasbord* (SMOER-gus-boerd). (A *smørgasbord* is a buffet of many different appetizers, salads, hot dishes, and desserts.)

The Vikings are said to have always brought back a variety of foods from their voyages. But they never brought enough of one kind for a full helping for everybody, so people at home only got a small taste of each! Today, a typical *smørgasbord* includes many kinds of fish, cold sliced meats, cheese, vegetables, molded fish and lettuce salads, breads, and a hot dish such as meatballs. Dessert may be fresh fruit, cold fruit soup, or rice pudding.

CUSTOMS

According to legend, *trolls* live in the mountains of Norway. These little creatures are said to be mean and ugly because they never come out of the mountains when the sun is shining. When I was in Norway, I bought a hand-carved wooden troll that was rubbing his stomach and smiling. I was told that when this troll wandered outside, the warm sun made him smile!

Sunshine always makes Norwegians smile— but when they are eating porridge, they are twice as happy! An old tale from Telemark, a southern province of Norway, says that each woman there was asked if she could make porridge. If the answer was "No," she was told, "You may as well pack up." In other words, if you couldn't make porridge, you were of no use! As this tale emphasizes, porridge is a very important part of the Norwegian diet.

Ordinary porridge, such as rice porridge (see page 16), is eaten for breakfast nearly every day by Norwegians, especially by those who work outdoors and in the country. Special porridges, such as *rommegrøt* (ROOM-uh-groet), are eaten as fancy desserts for holiday meals and Sunday dinners. Such porridges are often richer and harder to make than everyday porridge.

Another Norwegian favorite is rice pudding, a tasty dessert with a smooth texture and a rich flavor. You can eat it plain or with cinnamon and sugar. And you can add milk or cream or top it with berries. Although rice pudding can be eaten anytime, in Norway it is traditionally a Christmas and New Year's dish.

Some families always eat rice pudding at their Christmas Eve meal. In some households, an almond is placed in the pudding, and whoever finds it gets a little gift. That person is also supposed to have good luck and happiness in the new year. In other families, the person who gets the almond is in charge of ceremonies on Christmas Eve, which is when the Norwegians open their gifts.

You might want to start your own family tradition. If you have a family night, the person who finds the almond might choose something the whole family can enjoy, such as a game, a movie, or an outing.

Now that you know some of the foods and customs of Norway, try making your own Norwegian meals soon. Then go on to the best part—eating them!

This happy troll is busy cooking his favorite rice porridge for breakfast.

BEFORE YOU BEGIN

Cooking any dish, plain or fancy, is easier and more fun if you are familiar with its ingredients. Norwegian cooking makes use of some ingredients that you may not know. You should also be familiar with the special terms that will be used in various recipes in this book. Therefore, *before* you start cooking any of the dishes in this book, study the following "dictionary" of special ingredients and terms very carefully. Then read through the recipe you want to try from beginning to end.

Now you are ready to shop for ingredients and to organize the cookware you will need. Once you have assembled everything, you can begin to cook. It is also very important to read *The Careful Cook* on page 43 before you start. Following these rules will make your cooking experience safe, fun, and easy.

COOKING TERMS

boil — To heat a liquid over high heat until bubbles form and rise rapidly to the surface

brown — To cook food quickly in fat over high heat so that the surface turns an even brown

fold — To blend an ingredient with other ingredients by using a gentle overturning circular motion instead of by stirring or beating

hard-cook — To cook an egg in its shell until both the yolk and white are firm

knead — To work dough by pressing it with the palms, pushing it outward, and then pressing it over on itself

preheat — To allow an oven to warm up to a certain temperature before putting food in it

scald — To heat a liquid (such as milk) to a temperature just below its boiling point

shred — To tear or cut into small pieces, either by hand or with a grater

simmer — To cook over low heat in liquid kept just below its boiling point. Bubbles may occasionally rise to the surface.

SPECIAL INGREDIENTS

allspice — A spice similar to a mixture of cinnamon, nutmeg, and cloves. It can be substituted for any of these spices.

almond extract — A liquid used to give an almond flavor to food. It is made from oil extracted from the almond nut.

buttermilk — A milk product made from soured milk

cardamom seed — A spice from the ginger family, either whole or ground, that has a rich odor and gives food a sweet cool taste

cornmeal — A meal made from ground corn

cornstarch — A fine white starch made from corn, commonly used for thickening sauces and gravies. *(When you use cornstarch in a recipe, put the required amount of dry cornstarch in a cup and add just enough cold water to form a smooth, thin paste. Then add to the other ingredients. This method keeps the cornstarch from forming lumps when cooked in liquid.)*

dill — An herb whose seeds and leaves are both used in cooking. The flavor of the leaves is similar to that of parsley, and the flavor of the seeds resembles caraway seed.

gelatin — A clear, powdered protein substance used as a thickening agent

nutmeg — A fragrant spice, either whole or ground, that is often used in desserts

paprika — A red seasoning made from ground, dried pods of the *capsicum* pepper plant. It has a sweeter flavor than red pepper.

sorghum — A dark-colored syrup similar to molasses but with a stronger flavor

stone-ground whole wheat flour — A flour from wheat that is ground under a millstone. It is called whole wheat because the bran is not removed from the grain.

white pepper — A seasoning made from ground peppercorns. White pepper is used when black pepper would make the food look less appealing.

yeast — An ingredient used in baking that causes dough to rise up and become light and fluffy. Yeast is available in either small, white cakes called compressed yeast or in granular form called active dry yeast.

A NORWEGIAN MENU

Below is a simplified Norwegian menu plan that includes several Swedish, Danish, and Finnish recipes. The Norwegian and/or Swedish (S), Danish (D), and Finnish (F) names of the dishes are given, along with a guide on how to pronounce them. Two alternate dinner ideas are included. Recipes for the starred items can be found in this book.

ENGLISH	NORSKE	PRONUNCIATION GUIDE
MENU	MENY	MEH-nih
Breakfast	**Frokost**	**FRUH-kohst**
*Rice porridge	Risengrynsgrøt	REES-en-greens-groet
Soft-boiled eggs	Bløtkokt egg	BLOEHT-kokd ekg
Cheese	Ost	ohst
*Flatbread or rye crisp	Flatbrød eller knekkebrød	FLAHT-broeh el-luhr kuh-NIK-yuh-broeh
*Christmas bread, butter, and jam	Julebrød, smør, og syltetøi	YOO-luh-broeh, smoehr, oh SEEL-tih-toy
Lunch	**Lunsj**	**lunch**
*Potato soup	Potetsuppe	poh-TEHT-suh-puh
*Open-face sandwiches	Smørbrød	SMOEHR-broeh
*Finnish cookie sticks	Suomalaiset puikot (F)	SOO-oh-mah-lye-set POO-ee-cot

ENGLISH	NORSKE	PRONUNCIATION GUIDE
Snack	**Snack**	**snack**
Lefse with butter and sugar	Lefse med smør og sukker	LEHF-suh meh smoehr oh SOOH-kair
*Flatbread and cheese	Flatbrød og ost	FLAHT-broeh oh ohst
Fresh fruit	Frukt	frukt
*Whole wheat rusks and milk	Kavring og melk	KAH-vring oh melk
Dinner	**Middag**	**mee-DAHG**
I	I	
*Norwegian/Swedish meatballs	Kjøttkaker	SHET-kah-kair
	Køttbullar (S)	SHET-boh-lar
*Boiled potatoes	Kokte poteter	KOHK-teh poh-TEH-tuhr
*Peas	Erter	AR-tuhr
*Rice pudding	Rispudding	REES-puh-ding
	Risgrynskaka (S)	REES-grins-kah-kah
	Riskrem (D)	REES-krem
II	II	
*Baked cod	Ovnstekt torsk	UH-vehn-shtehkt torshk
*Finnish stewed potatoes	Muhennetut perunat (F)	MUH-henna-tut PER-un-at
*Danish pickled cucumbers	Syltede agurker (D)	SEEL-tih-duh ah-GOR-ker
*Fruit soup	Fruktsuppe	FRUKT-suh-puh

BREAKFAST/ Frokost

This rice porridge recipe is a simple one, and it does not take long to make. For a change of pace, however, you might want to try oatmeal or any commercial hot breakfast cereal fixed the Norwegian way. Just liven it up with raisins, cinnamon, brown sugar, honey, or thick cream.

In addition to porridge, the Norwegians eat many other foods for breakfast that turn it into a "mini-*smørgasbord*." You may choose any or all of the foods on the breakfast menu, but be sure to have some cheese. *Gjetost,* or goat's cheese, as well as flatbread and rye crisp can be found in most supermarkets. *Gjetost* has an unusual flavor, so buy only a small amount if you are tasting it for the first time.

Rice Porridge/ Risengrynsgrøt

4 cups milk
½ teaspoon salt
1 cup cooked white rice
2 teaspoons butter

1. Combine milk and salt in a saucepan and bring to a boil over medium heat.
2. Add rice and butter.
3. Boil for 15 minutes at medium heat, stirring constantly.
4. Cover and turn heat to low.
5. Simmer for 4 minutes, stirring occasionally.
6. Serve hot, sprinkled with sugar and cinnamon or with milk and 1 teaspoon butter.

Serves 4

Christmas bread makes a colorful holiday gift. For an extra festive touch, frost your *julebrød* with white icing and decorate it with sliced almonds. (Recipe on page 18.)

Christmas Bread/
Julebrød

Another treat that is delicious with breakfast is julebrød, *or Christmas bread. It makes wonderful toast. Making bread can be tricky at first, so try to have an experienced person help you. To simplify this recipe, use frozen white bread dough.*

2 tablespoons active dry yeast
1 tablespoon sugar
¼ cup warm water
2 cups milk
½ cup shortening
½ cup sugar
2 teaspoons salt
2 teaspoons ground cardamom seed
6½ cups all-purpose flour
1 cup candied red and green cherries
    or assorted candied fruit,
    cut in thirds
1 cup raisins
½ cup blanched almonds, finely
    chopped
    additional all-purpose flour
      (½ to 1½ cups)

1. Soften raisins by putting them in small amount of hot water. Prepare cherries by shaking them in a bag with a little flour. Set cherries and raisins aside.
2. In a glass measuring cup or a drinking glass, dissolve yeast and 1 tablespoon sugar in ¼ cup warm water.
3. In a saucepan, scald milk. Stir in shortening and let cool for 15 minutes.
4. When milk and shortening have cooled, pour into a big mixing bowl.
5. Add ½ cup sugar, salt, and ground cardamom seed to milk and shortening. Stir.
6. With a mixing spoon, stir in 2 cups flour, 1 cup at a time.
7. Add yeast, sugar, and water mixture. Stir.
8. Stir in 2 more cups flour. Then add candied fruit, raisins, and chopped almonds, mixing well.
9. Stir in 2½ cups of remaining flour, 1 cup at a time.
10. Turn dough out on a floured board and knead well. Use as much remaining flour as it takes to produce a springy,

elastic texture. (See kneading diagram.) Place dough in a greased bowl and cover with a damp cloth.

11. Put dough in a warm place (about 80°) or in a closed oven (turned off) with a pan of hot water on the bottom rack. Let dough rise until double. Punch down and let rise until double again.

12. Punch down and cut into 2 equal sections.

13. Knead well. Form round loaves and place them on a cookie sheet. Cover with a damp cloth and let rise.

14. Preheat the oven to 350°. (Be sure to remove the 2 loaves first if you have put them in the oven to rise!)

15. Bake loaves for about 35 minutes. (Tops should be golden brown.)

Makes 2 round loaves

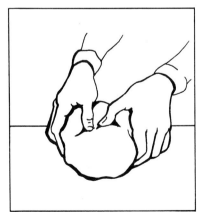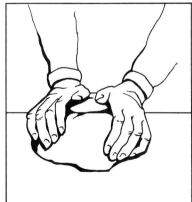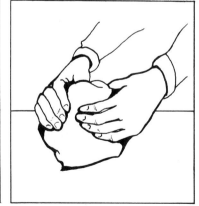

1. Form dough into a ball. 2. Press dough down with your palms. Then push it outward with the heel of your hand. 3. Fold and press dough over on itself. 4. Repeat Step 2, pressing dough down and pushing it outward.

LUNCH/
Lunsj

Most offices close at 3:00 P.M. in Norway's cities. The workers have a short coffee and sandwich break at noon and a late lunch or an early dinner at home after work. In the small villages and homes in the valleys, lunch is eaten around 12:00 or 1:00 P.M. Try the following Norwegian favorites for a delicious and filling lunch of your own.

Potato Soup/
Potetsuppe

4 medium-sized potatoes
1 onion
½ teaspoon salt
2 cups whole milk
2 tablespoons butter
½ tablespoon chopped fresh parsley
⅛ teaspoon pepper

1. Peel each potato and cut into 4 pieces.
2. Peel onion and chop it well. Put potatoes, onion, and salt in a heavy 2-quart saucepan. Pour water into the pan, covering vegetables.
3. Boil until a fork goes into potatoes easily (about 15 to 20 minutes). (Do not drain.) Then mash potatoes and onion in the pan.
4. Add milk slowly, stirring all the time. Allow soup to simmer while you add butter, parsley, and pepper.
5. Stir over medium heat until soup is smooth and hot.

Serves 4

A bowl of creamy potato soup and a green salad make a great light meal any time of day.

Open-Face Sandwiches/ Smørbrød

The open-face sandwich, which is a sandwich without a top, is very popular in Scandinavia. This sandwich can be made with many different ingredients, but it is always made in the same way— a leaf of lettuce is placed on bread or rye crisp, topped first with a piece of meat, a small fish, or a piece of cheese, and then with a small piece of decorative food called a garnish. As you can see, making open-face sandwiches is a good way to use up leftovers. It is also a good way in which to be creative—your sandwiches should not only taste good, they should look good, too.

Sandwich ingredients:

French-style white bread, cut in ⅜-inch slices, or rye crisp
softened butter
lettuce
fillings (meat, cheese, shrimp, sardines)
garnishes

The following ingredients can be used in various combinations as garnishes for at least 20 sandwiches. Use any leftovers in your next tossed green salad.

Garnishes:

1 tomato, unpeeled
1 lemon, unpeeled
1 cucumber, unpeeled
2 radishes
2 hard-cooked eggs
1 green pepper
paprika

To prepare garnishes:

1. Cut tomato into thin wedges about ¼ inch thick at the edge.
2. Wash lemon and cucumber thoroughly and use a sharp knife to slice them as thinly as possible. Make a slit up to the center of each slice. (The cut edges will be twisted in opposite directions when placed on a sandwich.)
3. Thinly slice radishes and hard-cooked eggs and clean out and cut green pepper in narrow strips about 2 inches long.

4. Sprinkle a bit of paprika on the yolks of some of the egg slices. Cover garnishes with plastic wrap and refrigerate until you are ready to assemble sandwiches.

Sandwich filling:

1 7-ounce tin of sardines (which will make about 7 sandwiches)
1 7-ounce can of tiny cooked shrimp (enough for 5 sandwiches)
boiled ham, thinly sliced (one slice per sandwich)
roast beef, thinly sliced (one slice per sandwich)
hard cheese such as cheddar or Swiss (two slices per sandwich)

You may use cold ham or beef from last night's meal. Or you can go to the meat market and have the butcher cut the number of slices you'll need. The slices must be cut as thinly as possible, but not so thin that they fall apart.

When you have gathered all the ingredients, you are ready to assemble the sandwiches. First spread a little butter over each slice of bread and cover the bread with a lettuce leaf. Then arrange the ham on the lettuce leaf so that there is a fold in the middle. Try folding the beef over once or forming it into a little roll. And use a variety of hard cheeses for eye and taste appeal.

Now you are ready to put the garnishes on the sandwiches. There is no "right way" to put the meat and garnishes together. The enjoyable part of sandwich-making is experimenting with different arrangements. Have fun!

Five tasty sandwich combinations:

1. 3 sardines, egg slice, green pepper strip, lemon twist
2. spoonful of shrimp, cucumber and lemon twisted together, radish slices
3. boiled ham, egg slice, tomato wedge, cucumber twist
4. roast beef, egg slice, tomato wedge, green pepper strip
5. cheese, tomato wedge, green pepper strip

Finnish Cookie Sticks/
Suomalaiset Puikot

1 cup butter, softened
½ cup sugar
1 egg
1 teaspoon almond extract
¼ teaspoon salt
3 cups all-purpose flour, sifted
3 eggs, beaten
3 or 4 tablespoons sugar (for coating)
1½ cups finely chopped almonds

1. Blend butter and ½ cup sugar until smooth and creamy.
2. Stir in egg, almond extract, and salt.
3. Add flour and work mixture with hands until it is a smooth dough.
4. Roll into long rolls about ½ to ¾ inch thick.
5. Cut into 2- to 3-inch pieces. Dip each in eggs, then in sugar, and then in almonds.
6. Bake on a greased cookie sheet at 350° for 8 to 10 minutes or until cookies are very light brown.

Makes 5 dozen cookies

Crunchy, almond-flavored cookie sticks are as pretty to serve as they are good to eat.

SNACK/
Snack

For a hearty after-school snack, you may want to try a little *lefse* or some flatbread and cheese with a piece of fruit. *Lefse* is a kind of soft, thin potato cake that is white with brown "freckles." It can be eaten plain or buttered, and when spread with butter *and* sprinkled with sugar, it's heavenly. *Lefse* can be found in most supermarkets. Norwegian flatbread is a thin, crisp waferlike bread. By itself it is quite bland, but with butter or a piece of cheese it makes a delicious snack. The following flatbread recipe is quite simple.

Flatbread can also be found in most supermarkets.

Kavring, or whole wheat rusks, is a dried bread snack that is crunchy and delicious. It was my favorite after-school snack when I was young, and I always had plenty of it. My dad and my grandmothers made fresh *kavring* nearly every week.

You can also snack on leftover rice pudding or fruit soup (which you will soon learn to make). These treats are just as good on the second or third day as on the first, and it's a nice change to eat them cold.

Spread with butter or topped with cheese, flatbread is a nutritious treat. For extra nutrition, add corn-meal to the dough.

Flatbread/
Flatbrød

For some tasty variations of this recipe, try making flatbread using only white flour or only rye flour. You can also substitute ⅔ cup cornmeal for ⅔ cup flour.

1⅓ cups stone-ground whole wheat flour
1⅓ cups all-purpose flour
¼ cup vegetable oil
1 teaspoon baking soda
½ teaspoon salt
¾ to 1 cup buttermilk

1. Combine first 5 ingredients in a bowl. Mix well.
2. Add only enough buttermilk to make a stiff dough.
3. Knead dough for 30 seconds on a well-floured surface (such as a board or tabletop).
4. Roll a medium-sized handful of dough (about ¼ cup) into a ball and then pat it down into a flat circle. (Cover remaining dough so it doesn't become too dry.)
5. With a floured stockinet-covered rolling pin and on a well-floured surface, roll dough into a very thin 10-inch circle. (If dough is sticking to the surface on which you are working, dust it with more flour.)
6. Place flatbread on an ungreased cookie sheet. (To make all of your flatbread pieces the same shape and size, score (mark with a deep line) dough circles with a knife, making triangles, squares, or whatever shapes you prefer. After baking, break flatbread along scored lines.)
7. Bake at 350° for 8 to 10 minutes. (Flatbread should be crisp and slightly brown around the edges.) Cool on wire rack and repeat with remaining dough.
8. Break into pieces and serve plain or with desired topping, such as butter or cheese.

Makes 9 circles

Whole Wheat Rusks/ Kavring

This recipe for kavring *is the same as that for whole wheat bread. So instead of making two pans of* kavring, *you can make two small loaves of bread and one pan of* kavring.

1 tablespoon active dry yeast
¼ cup brown sugar
1 cup warm water
2½ cups milk
⅓ cup shortening
¼ cup sorghum or molasses
1 tablespoon salt
1½ cups whole wheat flour
2½ cups all-purpose flour
additional whole wheat flour
(at least 4 cups)

1. In a small glass bowl or a large drinking glass, dissolve yeast and brown sugar in 1 cup warm water.
2. Scald milk in a saucepan. Turn off the burner under the pan and add shortening while milk is cooling.
3. When shortening-and-milk mixture has cooled for 15 minutes, pour into a large mixing bowl.
4. Add sorghum and salt to mixture.
5. With a wooden spoon, stir 1½ cups whole wheat flour and 2½ cups all-purpose flour into mixture, 1 cup at a time.
6. Stir in yeast mixture.
7. Stir in additional cups whole wheat flour, 1 cup at a time, until dough is of kneading consistency. (You may need up to 4 cups whole wheat flour.)
8. Turn out dough on a board dusted with whole wheat flour. Knead until dough is smooth and elastic.
9. Place in a greased mixing bowl. Cover with a damp cloth. Put in a warm place and let rise until double.
10. Punch down and form into narrow rolls about 1 inch wide and 2½ inches long. (Or form dough into 2 small loaves and the rest into narrow rolls.)
11. Place rolls close together in a greased 9- by 13-inch pan and loaves in two 3- by 6-inch pans. Let rise in a warm place until

double. While dough is rising, preheat the oven to 350°.

12. Bake for 30 minutes.

13. Remove rolls and bread from pans and let cool.

14. To make *kavring,* split rolls lengthwise by hand (so that they are roughedged), place halves in pans, and return to the oven to dry out very slowly. Turn on the oven at 225° for 2 or 3 periods of about 10 to 15 minutes each during drying process.

15. Store *kavring* in a tightly covered container.

Makes two pans of 40 kavring *buns each, or two loaves and one pan of 40* kavring.

The recipe for whole wheat rusks is large enough to make a loaf or two of bread in addition to *kavring.* Flavored with sorghum and brown sugar, *kavring* buns and bread are both delicious.

DINNER/ Middag

The evening meal is a special time for the family to be together. This meal is eaten any time between 6:30 and 7:30 P.M.

I have suggested a variety of healthy dishes to try for dinner. Whatever foods you choose to cook, serve them with pride. All the Norwegians whom I visited or stayed with took special care and pride in all food preparation. Cleanliness, accuracy in measuring, and fresh, good-quality ingredients are the three most important guidelines for the Norwegian cook, or for any cook! Remember these guidelines as you prepare the following dinner foods.

Baked Cod/ Ovnstekt Torsk

Fish is often served in Norway, and it is prepared in many ways. It can be poached in water, fried, or baked in milk.

6 cod fillets (thaw if frozen)
4 cups hot milk (enough to barely cover the fish)
6 teaspoons butter

1. Preheat the oven to 350°.
2. Grease a shallow baking dish or a 9- by 13-inch pan. Arrange fillets, placing them close together in the dish or pan. (Choose a baking container in which fillets will fit closely together.)
3. Pour enough hot milk over fish to barely cover fillets.
4. Top each fillet with teaspoon of butter. Bake for 20 minutes or until fish flakes easily when tested with a fork.

Serves 4 to 6

Cod baked in hot milk and butter is a simple but tasty dish. You can add sprigs of fresh green parsley for color.

Norwegian/Swedish Meatballs/ Kjøttkaker/Køttbullar(S)

Meatball ingredients:

**4 slices white bread
¾ cup hot milk
2 pounds ground beef
½ pound ground pork
2 eggs, beaten
¼ teaspoon nutmeg
¼ teaspoon pepper
⅛ teaspoon allspice
½ cup chopped onion
2 teaspoons salt
2 teaspoons shortening**

1. Soak bread in hot milk until milk is absorbed.
2. Combine all ingredients in a large bowl and mix thoroughly by hand.
3. Shape into small balls 1 inch in diameter. (A heaping tablespoon of meat makes about the right size meatball. It is easier to shape the balls if you wet your hands first.)

The ingredients for Norwegian and Swedish meatballs are the same: ground meat and onion are mixed with fresh eggs and bread and flavored with nutmeg and allspice.

4. **For Norwegian meatballs:** In a skillet, brown meatballs in 2 teaspoons hot shortening. Then place in a covered baking dish. Pour off fat but save drippings in the skillet for gravy.

Norwegian gravy ingredients:

2 tablespoons butter
2 tablespoons all-purpose flour
1 beef bouillon cube
1¼ cups boiling water

1. Preheat the oven to 325°.
2. Melt butter in the skillet with drippings from browning meatballs.
3. Stir in flour with a fork. Then get ready to add bouillon cube dissolved in 1¼ cups boiling water. It is best to add only a little of this liquid at first, stirring with a fork until mixture is a smooth paste. Then add rest of bouillon water a little at a time, stirring constantly to keep gravy smooth.
4. Pour over meatballs and bake 30 minutes in the covered baking dish.

4. **For Swedish meatballs:** Brown meatballs in 2 teaspoons hot shortening (about 2 minutes on each side). Reduce heat to low, cover pan, and simmer for 8 minutes. Remove meatballs and pour off fat, saving drippings in the skillet for gravy.

Swedish gravy ingredients:

1 cup light cream
1 tablespoon cornstarch
2 tablespoons cold water

1. Add cream to drippings in the skillet.
2. Blend cornstarch and water. Add to skillet mixture.
3. Stir over moderate heat until mixture comes to a boil. If necessary, season with salt and pepper.
4. Serve gravy with meatballs.

Serves 10

This recipe makes about 60 meatballs. Don't worry if you have leftovers because the meatballs are delicious warmed up.

Swedish meatballs with gravy make a delicious main course for a family dinner or a special occasion.

Boiled Potatoes/
Kokte Poteter

Parsley-buttered potatoes are served nearly every night in Norway. In the summer Norwegians grow their own parsley outside, and in the winter they grow this garnish in small pots inside near the window.

6 medium-sized potatoes
1 teaspoon salt
2 tablespoons butter
1 tablespoon chopped fresh parsley

1. Peel potatoes and place them in a pan of cold, salted water. (The water should just cover potatoes.)
2. Cover the pan and place over a high heat. Allow potatoes to boil until tender (about 15 to 20 minutes). When a fork goes into potatoes easily, drain off water. (Save it for some homemade soup or for the next time you make meatball gravy.)
3. Put the lid back on the pan and return to the stove to keep warm. (Make sure that the burner under the pan is off.) Add butter and parsley before serving.

Serves 6

Finnish Stewed Potatoes/
Muhennetut Perunat

4 medium-sized potatoes, thinly sliced
1¼ cups light cream
dash of nutmeg
1 teaspoon salt
½ teaspoon white pepper
1 tablespoon chopped fresh parsley

1. In a large, heavy saucepan, bring potatoes, cream, and nutmeg to a boil.
2. Immediately reduce heat to very low and simmer until potatoes are tender (about 30 minutes).
3. Sprinkle with salt and pepper and garnish with parsley.

Serves 4

Peas/
Erter

½ cup water
1 tablespoon butter
2 cups fresh or frozen peas
1 cup finely shredded lettuce
2 tablespoons chopped onion
1 tablespoon chopped fresh parsley
½ teaspoon salt
dash of pepper

1. In a saucepan, bring water and butter to a boil.
2. Add peas, lettuce, onion, parsley, salt, and pepper.
3. Cover and simmer 10 to 15 minutes.

Serves 4

Danish Pickled
Cucumbers/
Syltede Agurker

3 medium-sized cucumbers (about 6 inches long)
½ cup vinegar
½ cup water
2 tablespoons sugar
1 teaspoon salt
¼ teaspoon white pepper
chopped fresh parsley or dill

1. Slice cucumbers very thin and place in a dish.
2. Combine vinegar, water, sugar, salt, and pepper in another bowl. Mix well with a fork.
3. Pour over cucumbers, cover the bowl, and refrigerate at least 2 hours.
4. Garnish with chopped parsley or dill before serving.

Serves 6 to 8

Norwegian Rice Pudding/ Rispudding

This recipe can also be made in a slow cooker. Just combine all of the ingredients, pour into a lightly greased cooker, and cook on High for 1 to 2 hours or on Low for 4 to 6 hours. Remember to stir during the first 30 minutes.

½ **cup white rice, uncooked**
⅛ **teaspoon salt**
3 **tablespoons sugar**
4 **cups milk**

1. Combine rice, salt, sugar, and 1 cup milk in a large, heavy saucepan.
2. Stir often over very low heat until milk is absorbed. Add remaining milk, 1 cup at a time. (Let each cup be absorbed before adding the next.) Stir often and *do not boil.* (Total cooking time: 2 hours.)
3. Serve pudding hot or cold with cream and cinnamon and sugar.

Serves 4

Swedish Rice Pudding/ Risgrynskaka

1 **cup white rice, uncooked**
1 **tablespoon butter**
1 **cup water**
5 **cups milk**
1 **teaspoon salt**
1 **tablespoon sugar**
2 **eggs**
⅓ **cup raisins**
   grated lemon rind (to taste)

1. Place rice in a sieve and scald by pouring boiling water over it.
2. Melt one half of butter and add rice and water to it. Boil until water disappears (10 to 15 minutes).
3. Add milk and cook slowly until rice is tender (about 45 minutes).
4. Stir in salt, sugar, and remaining butter.
5. Add eggs and raisins. Stir well.
6. Stir in lemon rind and pour into a buttered baking dish. Bake at 400° for 45 minutes. Serve hot or cold.

Serves 6

Danish rice pudding served with raspberry sauce is sure to win smiles of approval.

Danish Rice Pudding/ Riskrem

2 envelopes unflavored gelatin
½ cup sugar
½ cup water
½ teaspoon salt
2 cups milk
1½ cups cooked white rice
2 teaspoons vanilla extract
¼ cup chopped almonds
1 cup chilled whipping cream

1. In a saucepan, heat gelatin, sugar, water, and salt. Stir constantly until gelatin is dissolved (about 1 minute).
2. Stir in milk, rice, vanilla, and almonds.
3. Place the saucepan in a bowl of ice water, stirring occasionally for about 15 minutes. (Mixture should form a slight lump when dropped from a spoon.)
4. Beat whipping cream until stiff and fold into rice mixture.
5. Pour into an ungreased 1½-quart mold. Cover and chill until set (about 3 hours).

6. Turn out and serve cold with Raspberry Sauce.

Serves 8

Raspberry Sauce

1 10-ounce package frozen raspberries, thawed
½ cup apple or currant jelly
1 tablespoon cold water
1½ teaspoons cornstarch

1. In a saucepan, bring raspberries (with syrup) and jelly to a boil.
2. Combine water and cornstarch in a bowl. Then stir into raspberries.
3. Bring to a boil again, stirring constantly.
4. Boil and stir for one minute.
5. Serve warm sauce on top of *cold* pudding.

Serves 8

Cinnamon sticks add a spicy tang to Norwegian fruit soup.

Fruit Soup/
Fruktsuppe

This soup is cool, spicy, and refreshing.

1-pound package unpitted prunes
½ pound (1½ cups) raisins
2 cinnamon sticks
6 cups water
4 ounces (1 cup) dried apricots
1 8¾-ounce can unsweetened
      cherries and juice
3 tablespoons quick-cooking tapioca
¼ cup sugar

1. Put prunes, raisins, cinnamon sticks, and water in a large, heavy kettle. Bring to a boil, then reduce heat and simmer about 30 minutes or until prunes and raisins are soft.

2. Add apricots and cook for 10 minutes or until they are plump and soft.

3. Pour off liquid from cooked fruit into another kettle. (You may need help from a friend when you do this.) Add juice from cherries to liquid. Then add tapioca and sugar. Cook over a medium heat, stirring often, until tapioca is *clear.* The juice should be thick by this time. (You will have to cook mixture for at least 30 minutes to get clear tapioca and thickened juice.)

4. Add thickened juice and cherries to fruit. Stir. You can add slices of oranges and lemons to this mixture for color. Serve while warm, or eat cold.

Serves 12

A NORWEGIAN TABLE

When the table is set and the *torsk* is done to a turn, you are likely to hear the Norwegian cook say, *"Vær så god!"* This is a phrase that has many meanings and many uses. It is often used at mealtime when the mother calls the family to eat. Then it means "come on" or "here it is."

The table that the family comes to is a treat indeed. The Norwegians take great pride not only in the preparation of food but also in the table arrangements. Beautiful hand-woven table runners are often used instead of full tablecloths. Fresh flowers are on the table in many homes every day in the warmer months of the year. People in the small villages grow their own flowers, and people in the cities buy them at the outdoor flower markets. A single rose or a few daffodils can really help to make mealtime a happy occasion.

At the end of a meal, it is good to show that you have enjoyed the pleasant table setting and the good food. One of my fondest memories is of the time that I stayed with friends in Haugesund, a city on the south-western coast of Norway. After every meal (even after breakfast!) the children went over to their mother, shook her hand, and said, *"Takk for mat"* (thank you for the food), or *"Mange takk"* (many thanks). Good cooking is an art, and it is nice to be remembered for your work with a simple thank you.

And so I invite you to offer a Norwegian meal to your family. If you take time and pride in the preparation and serving of the food, I am sure that your family will reward your efforts with a hearty *"Tusen takk!"* (A thousand thanks!).

THE CAREFUL COOK

Whenever you cook, there are certain safety rules you must always keep in mind. Even experienced cooks follow these rules when they are in the kitchen.

1. Always wash your hands before handling food.
2. Thoroughly wash all raw vegetables and fruits to remove dirt, chemicals, and insecticides.
3. Use a cutting board when cutting up vegetables and fruits. Don't cut them up in your hand! And be sure to cut in a direction *away* from you and your fingers.
4. Long hair or loose clothing can easily catch fire if brought near the burners of a stove. If you have long hair, tie it back before you start cooking.
5. Turn all pot handles toward the back of the stove so that you will not catch your sleeve or jewelry on them. This is especially important when younger brothers and sisters are around. They could easily knock off a pot and get burned.

6. Always use a pot holder to steady hot pots or to take pans out of the oven. Don't use a wet cloth on a hot pan because the steam it produces could burn you.
7. Lift the lid of a steaming pot with the opening away from you so that you will not get burned.
8. If you get burned, hold the burn under cold running water. Do not put grease or butter on it. Cold water helps to take the heat out, but grease or butter will only keep it in.
9. If grease or cooking oil catches fire, throw baking soda or salt at the bottom of the flame to put it out. (Water will *not* put out a grease fire.) Call for help and try to turn all the stove burners to "off."

METRIC CONVERSION CHART

WHEN YOU KNOW		MULTIPLY BY	TO FIND	
MASS (weight)				
ounces	(oz)	28.0	grams	(g)
pounds	(lb)	0.45	kilograms	(kg)
VOLUME				
teaspoons	(tsp)	5.0	milliliters	(ml)
tablespoons	(Tbsp)	15.0	milliliters	
fluid ounces	(oz)	30.0	milliliters	
cup	(c)	0.24	liters	(l)
pint	(pt)	0.47	liters	
quart	(qt)	0.95	liters	
gallon	(gal)	3.8	liters	
TEMPERATURE				
Fahrenheit	(°F)	5/9 (after	Celsius	(°C)
temperature		subtracting 32)	temperature	

COMMON MEASURES AND THEIR EQUIVALENTS

3 teaspoons = 1 tablespoon

8 tablespoons = ½ cup

2 cups = 1 pint

2 pints = 1 quart

4 quarts = 1 gallon

16 ounces = 1 pound

INDEX

ABOUT THE AUTHOR

Author **Sylvia Munsen** is a third-generation Norwegian-American. Raised in Story City, Iowa, a community of Norwegian descendants, she was taught to treasure her ethnic heritage. She grew up eating many of the delicious foods included in this book and singing Norwegian folk songs with her grandmother.

Munsen graduated from St. Olaf College in Northfield, Minnesota, where she earned a degree in music education and was a member of the St. Olaf choir. She also studied Norwegian language and literature at the University of Oslo International Summer School. Afterwards she traveled throughout Norway, visiting friends and relatives in Bergen, Rosendal, Haugesund, and Stavanger. Munsen was able to share her knowledge of Norwegian folk songs, dances, tales, and art with children from kindergarten to the sixth grade when she later worked as an elementary music teacher in Osseo, Minnesota.

Since that time, Munsen has earned a doctorate in music education from the University of Illinois. She has been an instructor in music education and piano at Frostburg (Maryland) State College and in 1982 was appointed assistant professor of music and chair of the music education department at the University of Puget Sound in Tacoma, Washington.

easy menu *ethnic* cookbooks

Cooking the **CHINESE** Way
Cooking the **ENGLISH** Way
Cooking the **FRENCH** Way
Cooking the **ITALIAN** Way
Cooking the **JAPANESE** Way
Cooking the **MEXICAN** Way
Cooking the **NORWEGIAN** Way
Cooking the **SPANISH** Way

Lerner Publications Company
241 First Avenue North, Minneapolis, Minnesota 55401

ACKNOWLEDGMENTS: The illustrations are reproduced through the courtesy of: p. 2, The Danish Tourist Board; pp. 4, 26, 31, 38, 40, Burch Communications, Inc.; p. 8, Norwegian National Tourist Office; p. 17, RHODES Frozen Baking Dough; p. 21, Campbell Soup Company; p. 34, National Live Stock & Meat Board. Cover photograph courtesy of RHODES Frozen Baking Dough.